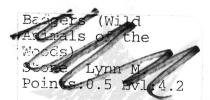

BADGERS

WILD ANIMALS OF THE WOODS

Lynn M. Stone

The Rourke Press, Inc.
Vero Beach, Florida 32964

PHOTO CREDITS
©Breck Kent: page 4; © Lynn M. Stone: cover, title page, pages 7,
10, 18, 21; © Tom Ulrich: pages 8, 12,13; © Tom and Pat Leeson:
pages 15, 17

Library of Congress Cataloging-in-Publication Data

Stone, Lynn M.
    Badgers / Lynn Stone.
        p. cm. — (Wild Animals of the woods)
    Includes index.
    ISBN 1-57103-094-8
    1. Badgers—North America—Juvenile literature.
[1. Badgers.]   I. Title II. Series: Stone, Lynn M. Wild Animals of
the woods.
QL737.C25S73 1995
599.74' 447—dc20   94–46897
                                                        CIP
                                                        AC

Printed in the USA

TABLE OF CONTENTS

BADGERS

The badger is a long-furred, four-footed digging "machine." In almost no time at all, this member of the weasel family can dig itself out of view.

A badger doesn't have a shovel, of course, but it may have the next best things—long claws and powerful shoulders and legs.

The badger's curious name may have come from the white mark, or "badge," on its forehead.

Dirt and dust fly as a badger digs out a burrow

HOW THEY LOOK

The handsome badger is silver-gray with black and white trim.

Its body is quite flat, and it has short legs. A badger hustles along low to the ground like a little moving carpet.

A big badger can be more than two feet long. Its short, bushy tail adds up to six more inches of length.

Badgers weigh from 8 to 25 pounds. Most weigh 10 to 12 pounds.

The silvery gray badger may have been named for the white "badge" on its forehead

WHERE THEY LIVE

Badgers generally live in dry, open areas of the West. Prairie, desert, and even pasturelands can be good badger **habitats** (HAB uh tats), or homes.

Badgers can be found from northern Alberta and southern British Columbia south to Ohio, central Mexico and Baja, California.

Badgers sometimes dig tunnels nine feet deep and as long as thirty feet.

Badgers live in several habitats throughout much of the West

HOW THEY ACT

Badgers are usually **nocturnal** (nahk TUR nul)—
they are active at night. A hungry badger, though,
will prowl about during the day. A badger may
choose to make den repairs in daylight, too.

Badgers don't sleep winter away in **hibernation**
(hi ber NAY shun). They slow down in cold weather,
however, and often nap for several days.

Young badgers may travel several miles looking
for a place to dig a den. Adults stay fairly close to
their burrows.

A badger leaves its den on an
early evening to begin hunting

A badger snarls as a rattlesnake approaches its den

This badger's home is a meadow near a farm

PREDATOR AND PREY

Badgers are **predators** (PRED uh tors), or hunting animals. They kill smaller animals, such as rodents, birds, lizards, snakes and insects, all or which are the badger's **prey** (PRAY).

Badgers eat mostly ground squirrels. A hungry, hunting badger will sometimes dig up several ground squirrel burrows in its search for food.

Adult badgers have no enemies. Young badgers can be prey for eagles and other large predators.

A badger brings home a ground squirrel

BADGER BABIES

A mother badger bears a **litter** (LIH ter) of one to five babies in the spring. Baby badgers are born in a nest of dry grass inside the burrow.

Baby badgers leave home early. At about two months of age, they move some distance from the home burrow.

A female badger may have her first litter when she is just a year old.

A captive badger can live for at least 26 years.

Young badgers play outside their burrow

THE BADGER'S COUSINS

Scientists call members of the weasel family—weasels, skunks, otters, wolverines, martens, fishers and badgers—mustelids.

Mustelids are meat-eating mammals with thick, soft fur and rather short **muzzles** (MUH zuls). Most mustelids produce a strong odor.

The badgers and their cousins live in a wide variety of habitats. Sea otters live in the ocean. Martens like trees and minks love shorelines.

The tree-loving pine marten is a cousin of the ground-loving badger

BADGERS AND PEOPLE

Badgers have earned people's respect because they are powerful and quite fearless. The University of Wisconsin's athletic teams are known as Badgers.

People once used badger fur for shaving brushes. Small amounts of badger fur are still used as trimming on clothes.

Farmers sometimes kill badgers by accident when badgers eat food that was poisoned to kill coyotes. Farmers generally like badgers because they help to keep the number of rodents down.

The badger's willingness to fight has earned it most people's respect

THE BADGER'S FUTURE

Badgers live over a wide part of North America. They disappeared from some places as their habitat was destroyed. But on the whole, badgers seem to be doing well.

Badgers are moving eastward into new "neighborhoods" where they never lived in the past. Badgers now live in most of Ohio and they're increasing in southeast Ontario.

Glossary

habitat (HAB uh tat) — the kind of place in which an animal lives, such as grassland

hibernation (hi ber NAY shun) — the deep, sleeplike state in which certain animals survive the winter

litter (LIH ter) — a group of babies born together by the same mother

muzzle (MUH zul) — an animal's jaws and nose, its snout

nocturnal (nahk TUR nul) — active at night

predator (PRED uh tor) — an animal that kills other animals for food

prey (PRAY) — an animal that is hunted by another for food

INDEX